Push and Pull

Cody Crane

Content Consultant

Elizabeth Case DeSantis, M.A. Elementary Education
Julia A. Stark Elementary School, Stamford, Connecticut

Reading Consultant

Jeanne M. Clidas, Ph.D.
Reading Specialist

Children's Press®

An Imprint of Scholastic Inc.

Library of Congress Cataloging-in-Publication Data
Names: Crane, Cody, author.
Title: Push and pull/by Cody Crane.
Other titles: Rookie read-about science.
Description: New York, NY: Children's Press, an imprint of Scholastic Inc., [2019] | Series: Rookie read-about science | Includes index.
Identifiers: LCCN 2018027646| ISBN 9780531134108 (library binding) | ISBN 9780531138045 (pbk.)
Subjects: LCSH: Force and energy–Juvenile literature. | Power (Mechanics)–Juvenile literature.
Classification: LCC QC73.4 .C73 2019 | DDC 531/.6—dc23

Produced by Spooky Cheetah Press
Design: Brenda Jackson
Digital Imaging: Bianca Alexis
Creative Direction: Judith E. Christ for Scholastic Inc.
© 2019 by Scholastic Inc. All rights reserved.

Published in 2019 by Children's Press, an imprint of Scholastic Inc.

Printed in Heshan, China   62

1 2 3 4 5 6 7 8 9 10 R 28 27 26 25 24 23 22 21 20 19

Scholastic Inc., 557 Broadway, New York, NY 10012

Photographs ©:cover: iridi/iStockphoto; back cover: Robert Daly/Getty Images; 2-3: Brian Kinney/Shutterstock; 5: fotoslaz/Shutterstock; 7: Robert Daly/Getty Images; 9: damedeeso/iStockphoto; 10: Edward Slater/Getty Images; 12-13: Lane Oatey/Blue Jean Images/Getty Images; 15: Doug Lemke/Shutterstock; 17: avid_creative/iStockphoto; 18: ImagesBazaar/Getty Images; 20-21: Soloviova Liudmyla/Shutterstock; 22: Kris Timken/Getty Images; 25: Neil Lockhart/Dreamstime; 27: Daniel Milchev/Getty Images; 28 cardboard: nito/Shutterstock; 28 cardboard: sripfoto/Shutterstock; 28 scissors: Vyacheslav Ryaschikov/Shutterstock; 28 tape: Luis Santos/Shutterstock; 28 books: tanuha2001/Shutterstock; 28 cars: Tatiana Popova/Shutterstock; 29 top: mike mols/Shutterstock; 29 bottom: DonSmith/Alamy Images; 30 bottom: fotoslaz/Shutterstock; 30 center: Neil Lockhart/Dreamstime; 30 top: Lane Oatey/Blue Jean Images/Getty Images; 31 bottom: Soloviova Liudmyla/Shutterstock; 31 center: ImagesBazaar/Getty Images; 31 top: fotoslaz/Shutterstock; 32: PM Images/Getty Images.

Table of Contents

Chapter 1

Ready, Set, Go!

How do you get something with wheels, like this shopping cart, rolling? You give it a **push**! All things need a push or a **pull** to get them moving.

Even you need a push or a pull to move. Your muscles push and pull your body when you run, swim, and jump.

Which part of this superhero's body is pushing as he jumps?

Pushes and pulls are all around us. The wind blowing over the ocean pushes the water. That creates waves. Waves can then push surfboarders.

How does the speed of the wind affect the size of waves?

9

Chapter 2

How Will It Move?

A push or a pull can be big or small. Heavier things need a bigger push to get them moving.

Does this rocket need a big or a little push to get off the ground?

Things can be pushed and pulled in different **directions**.

What
happens
when a rope
is pulled in
opposite
directions?

How something moves can be the result of lots of pushes and pulls. Roller coasters are one example. They have plenty of twists and turns.

What other machines move with the help of many different pushes and pulls?

Chapter 3

Making a Change

Some things are already moving when they get pushed or pulled.

How will the ball's motion change after it is hit?

17

The new push or pull can change the direction an object is moving in. It can also change its **speed**.

If the yellow bumper car hits the green one, how might the directions they were moving in change?

How might the speed of the yellow car change?

You can time how fast something moves with a **stopwatch**. It helps you see how a push or a pull slows something down . . . or speeds it up.

What push or pull activities can you time with a stopwatch?

Chapter 4

Slowing Down

A push or a pull can stop
something that is moving, too.
This goalie pushes with her
hands to stop the soccer ball.

Friction is a type of pull. It slows down things that are moving.
It can also bring them to a stop.

How is
this horse
using friction
to come to
a stop?

25

Friction happens when two things rub against each other. Try rubbing the palms of your hands together. Can you feel the pulling force of friction?

How would friction affect this skateboarder rolling down the ramp?

What are some things you do each day that need a push or a pull?

Toy Car Race

Can you make a toy car go faster using a ramp?

Remember to ask an adult for help with this activity.

1. Cut a long piece of cardboard. Prop up one end with books or a chair. Use tape to hold your ramp in place.

2. Give a toy car a gentle push on a flat surface. Watch how fast it goes.

3. Give the car a gentle push from the top of your ramp. Did it go faster than before?

What Happened?

Things roll downhill. So they do not need a big push, like they would on a flat surface, to get going.

directions (duh-**rek**-shuhnz): the ways something is facing or paths along which it moves

- *Kids playing tug-of-war pull in opposite* **directions***.*

friction (**frik**-shuhn): the force that works against motion when two things rub together

- *A horse's hooves digging into dirt creates* **friction***.*

pull

pull (puhl): a motion that draws one object toward another

- *A* **pull** *on a shopping cart moves it backward.*

push (push): the act of pressing on an object to move it away or ahead

- *A **push** on a shopping cart moves it forward.*

push

---

speed (speed): quickness in movement

- *After bumper cars crash, their **speed** may slow.*

---

stopwatch (stahp-wahch): a tool that can be started and stopped to measure time

- *A **stopwatch** helps measure how fast something moves.*

Facts for Now

Visit this Scholastic website for more information on force, and to download the Reader's Guide for this series: **http://www.factsfornow. scholastic.com** Enter the keywords **Push Pull**

About the Author

Cody Crane is an award-winning children's science writer. She lives in Texas with her husband and son.